THE OXBRIDGE LAW INTERVIEW TINY HANDBOOK

GETTING INTO OXFORD AND CAMBRIDGE LAW

LEO MILES

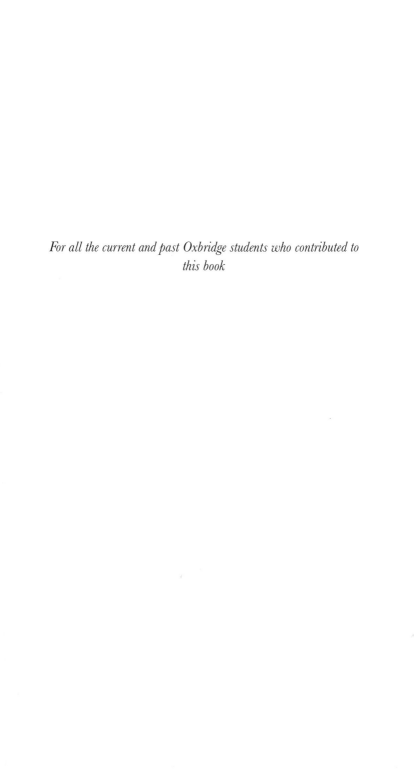

For all the current and past Oxbridge students who contributed to this book

CONTENTS

PREFACE

Hello there! Nice to meet you.

Welcome to *The Oxbridge Law Interview Tiny Handbook*! Thank you for taking a chance on this book. Before we get started, let's clarify what exactly this book is for and how you should use it.

Obviously, this book will help prepare you for Oxbridge law interviews. But how are we going to do that?

While the exact details of the questions cannot be predicted, there have been similar topics in their scenario questions that you should prepare for. This book will provide ample examples and explanations to build your confidence.

What the *Tiny Handbook* will do is help you gain the skills needed to ace the interviews, no matter what is thrown at you.

So the focus of this book is to help you develop the right way of thinking.

The structure of each main chapter is going to look like this.

1. Introduction: This is where the frameworks and

structure of your answer will be concisely explained. Once you're done with the whole book, this section can allow you to quickly refresh yourself with the concepts.

2. <u>Examples:</u> Here, we'll look at good representations of past interview questions and work through the right way to approach them.

This book has been written from information collected over two years. Sources include questions from past law interviews, books written by current Oxbridge professors, and LLB Law readings.

Before we begin, one last clarification. Typically there are two types of law interviews, scenario and case interviews. The scenario interview is when the tutors give you a hypothetical scenario to analyze, often verbally on the spot. The case interview is when they give you a case to look at (usually presented to you as a pre-reading before your interview).

This book targets the scenario section of the law interview, not the case interview. The scenarios are what trips students up the most, especially since it's seen as rather unpredictable and requires quick thinking.

But don't worry! After reading through this book, you'll be able to go into your interviews feeling much more prepared and ready.

So let's jump into it.

A FEW TIPS FOR YOUR INTERVIEW

Don't skip this section! After reading through this section, picture yourself on the day of your interview and get into that mindset before continuing.

An important thing to remember for the interview is to always vocalize your thoughts. But your thinking must be clear, concise, and structured. This book will help you develop that skill.

You don't need to know any fancy legal lingo, and you're not expected to. Tutors want to know how you respond to adversity by providing you with unexpected questions. They also want to make sure you can flourish during tutorials, so making sure you ask the right questions helps emulate a good tutorial. Even if you may not know much right now, you must show the ability to be guided and to be adaptable.

Once you are given your scenario verbally, try not to panic. Hopefully, you've built up your skills from reading this book to know exactly how to structure and deliver a strong answer.

Note-taking can help you keep track of the questions

the tutor asks you. This comes into play, especially when more elements are added and the question becomes more complicated.

- Always ask if it's okay to take notes before your interview begins. You'll have to flex your memorization skills if it's not allowed.

Remember that it's okay to ask any clarifying questions if you're confused or unclear on the details. As you work through your answer, you can stop and ask a question at any time.

The pressure of constantly being questioned and countered may fluster you. Just because you feel like you're being pushed to the max, it doesn't mean you're performing poorly. And just because your tutor tries to pick apart your argument doesn't mean you're wrong.

However, it's important to know when your tutor is trying to test you (by seeing how you continue to defend your argument) and when your tutor is trying to steer you in the right direction (because you went off track or are otherwise incorrect). More practice with actual cases and the scenarios in this book will better help you figure out the difference.

ANSWER STRUCTURE

T his section will help you better understand the framework underlying the worked-out answers later in the book. We'll start by explaining several basic concepts and then show you how to apply them using simple scenarios.

———

Category

Once you are verbally given your scenario, the first thing you need to do is identify the category it falls into. Every following chapter of this book represents a category with further subcategories to outline how to approach the question.

Read through each introduction carefully before diving into the guided question explanations. That way, you have the tools to better understand why answers are structured the way they are.

If you have limited time to study before your interview, the most important chapters are the first three, covering

Breach of Duty, **Causation Part One**, and **Causation Part Two**. These three parts should give you a good foundation, even if other questions are asked during your interview.

Once you establish the category, you can think back to the specific sections of this book to help guide you through the scenario. The reference table at the end of this section summarizes the main categories covered in the *Tiny Handbook*.

———

The Chain

Every scenario can be simplified into a chain diagram. Throughout the book, most scenarios will be represented in text and a chain.

Here's an example.

Tutor: Stella stepped on a rock and fell back, hitting her head.

Chain: **steps on rock -> falls + head injury**

The chain makes it easier to focus on the key facts. You don't have to use it, but it's a great tool when you're taking notes (written down or mentally) while the interviewer is speaking. When there are multiple people involved in the scenario, you could mark down names too.

———

The Answer Structure

For the main part of the book, answers will follow the

same general structure. The rest of the questions covered will have more variable structures.

Most of the time, your verbal answer should ideally be structured in two parts.

1. Identify possible answers
2. For each answer:

A) Plan out the heart of your answer (using the correct category, stating assumptions, asking questions, etc.)

B) Analyze the scenario, and mention both sides of your analysis if applicable. The two sides of the analysis may be hypotheticals or different perspectives.

Hypotheticals: This is where you give different answers based on hypothetical scenarios (ex. If the cat was brown, it ate the mouse. If the cat was black, then it ate the fish).

Perspectives: This is where you discuss the implications of two opposing stances (ex. If we establish the cat ate the fish, then we would need to regulate all outdoor cats. If we established the fish died on its own, then we wouldn't need to waste resources on enforcing new regulations).

———

The analysis is obviously the most important part of your answer.

- If you get stuck, try this method: Ask yourself, "Would B happen if A didn't happen?"

Why do we ask that key question? Because that's the crux of legal causation.

To simplify the concept, we'll use an easy example.

Imagine I yelled out the window, and then the birds on the fence flew away.

> yell out the window -> birds flew away

On the surface, it looks like the birds flew away because of my loud voice. But if we can establish that even if I didn't yell, the birds would still fly away, then it's not my doing.

> ~~yell out the window~~ -> birds flew away

Maybe the birds were scared of a dog running over, or there was a disturbance in the air making them want to leave. There are countless other explanations.

———

Put It All Together: Example Scenario

Let's run through a quick Breach of Duty example using all the points mentioned above.

Firstly, here's the question.

Tutor: Selena is drunk driving, and she doesn't notice Cassie's car driving right ahead. She crashes into it, causing Cassie's car to swerve off the road and hit a tree. Is Selena responsible for Cassie's resulting injuries?

The chain could be:

Selena drunk driving -> Cassie's car crash -> injuries

TIP: The chain only shows the main facts provided, and it's there for you to refer to as you work through your answer. Your chain may have more or less information, depending on what you want to remember.

1. Possible answers

The possible answers are yes, Selena's responsible, and no, she's not. While you may jump to say it's likely she's responsible, let's look at both scenarios closely.

2. Should Selena be liable for Cassie's car accident?

A) As a driver, Selena has a duty to abide by the relevant laws. Drunk driving is against the law. However, whether this is relevant when talking about liability for Cassie's injuries requires further inquiry.

B) We can attempt to find other alternate explanations for Cassie's crash. If we can show that Cassie's car would've swerved even without Selena's involvement, there's an argument that Selena should be off the hook.

- Perhaps Cassie lost traction when she drove on ice, or she had a medical condition that led to her losing control. In situations like these, Selena's drunk driving wouldn't be to blame, at least not wholly.
- Now let's mention the other possibility. If it's established that Cassie would not have crashed without Selena's involvement, Selena would be 100% liable and have to compensate Cassie for her injuries.

In this step, you can ask your interviewer questions to see if you can come to a straightforward answer.

A Reference Table

The table below includes every category and sub-category in the main part of the book. You might find it helpful to refer to as you continue reading.

Category	Sub	Key Ideas
Breach of Duty	Doctors	Have a responsibility to act in the best interests of their patients
	Drivers	Must drive at the expected standards of an experienced and skilled driver
	Employees	Have a responsibility to perform work to industry standards
	Employers	Must provide a safe work environment for employees
	Strangers	Do not generally have to help other strangers
Causation Part One	Hypotheticals	Not relevant
	Unforeseeable Events	Not relevant
	Vulnerable Victims	Are prioritized in the legal system
Causation Part Two	Sufficient Concurrent Causes	Everyone is liable
	Cumulative Concurrent Causes	Everyone is liable
	Evidence-Related	No liability
Lost Opportunities	>50% chance pre-incident	No liability because the difference is not is not significant enough
	<50% chance pre-incident	Liable

PART I

BREACH OF DUTY

INTRODUCING BREACH OF DUTY

T he law has maintained that certain roles have responsibilities the court will enforce. Those roles may be certain professions, familial relationships, or otherwise established relationships.

If someone in that role breaches their duty, the law will hold them responsible.

For our purposes, we'll focus on just a few roles.

1. <u>Doctor-Patient</u>: A doctor has a professional obligation to treat their patients to an established medical standard.
2. <u>Driver-Pedestrian</u>: Anybody operating a motor vehicle must be mindful of pedestrians.
3. <u>Employer-Employee</u>: Employers have a duty towards their employees based on the established industry standards.
4. <u>Stranger-Stranger</u>: Whether two people who aren't family have a duty towards each other depends on several key factors.

Keep in mind that these roles will come up again within other chapters as well. So by the end of this book, you'll be very familiar with these concepts.

Now, let's delve into the details of each role by looking at scenarios that may come up in your interviews!

DOCTORS, DRIVERS

INTRODUCING DUTIES OF DOCTORS, DRIVERS

The following two scenarios concern two duties you should know.

Professions such as doctors and lawyers have professional standards they must uphold. Road users, including drivers, also have duties they must abide by.

Here's what you need to remember for your interview. Doctors must:

- Have their patients' best interests at heart
- Inform patients of any risks that will impact their medical decision-making
- Perform their duties to the established professional medical standards

Road users must:

- Take reasonable care to prevent damage to others, including other road users, passengers, and pedestrians
- Drive at the standard of an experienced and skilled driver

- Follow the laws

Knowing these duties will help guide your questions to the tutor as you attempt to come up with a solid answer.

Instead of explaining how to approach a scenario, let's jump right into working through an example. That way, you'll immediately familiarize yourself with the format of this book. Also, it's easier to memorize a framework when you see it used in action.

The rest of the scenarios will follow the same style.

WRONG PRESCRIPTION

Category: Doctors, Drivers

Tutor: Anna is a doctor who is having a stressful day. She accidentally prescribes the wrong medication to her patient, Derek. After leaving the appointment, Derek gets into his car and starts driving home. He begins to feel dizzy, his vision blurs, and all that cumulates to him hitting a pedestrian walking across the road. The pedestrian dies. Who is responsible for the pedestrian's death?

To simplify the scenario, let's represent it with the below chain.

doctor (Anna) wrong meds -> patient (Derek) drives -> kills pedestrian

The ideal structure for your answer was mentioned in

the Answer Structure section, so let's use that to guide our thinking here.

1. *Possible answers*

The potential people responsible are Anna and Derek.

2. *Analyzing Anna, Derek*

We need to analyze both Anna and Derek in turn.

A) ANNA: As a doctor, Anna is reasonably expected to do her job correctly. Prescribing the wrong medication is a normal course of her expected work and is therefore a breach of duty.

B) To determine whether Anna bears any responsibility for the outcome, we need to know whether Derek would've driven like that even without the effects of the wrong medicine.

- If he would have driven wildly anyway, Anna is off the hook. She will not be held responsible and you can pinpoint Derek as the final answer.

You can ask the interviewer for clarification or directly say, "I'm going to assume that the patient wouldn't normally drive so erratically without the influence of the wrong medication."

The tutor will help lead you to follow their line of thinking.

- But let's say Derek's driving was indeed impacted by the medicine, and he has always been a very stable driver.

A) DEREK: As a driver, Derek has a responsibility to promote the safety of other road users. So the caveat here is whether Derek was aware he was feeling unwell and shouldn't be driving.

B) The answer would determine how we can split the responsibility between Anna and Derek.

- If Derek couldn't tell he was dizzy and unfit to drive, he wouldn't be liable for the death of the pedestrian.
- If Derek was aware he wasn't feeling good, he breached his duty as a road user. A reasonable driver would stop as soon as he started feeling dizzy. As the direct cause, Derek could be 75% responsible and Anna could bear the remaining 25%.

The most common percentage breakdowns are 50/50, 75/25, and 100/0. Hover around those numbers and you'll be fine. You're probably not going to be asked about a monetary remedy (where numbers get more specific), but just in case, there's an extra section in the last chapter of this book. It's worth the read.

BEFORE WE CONTINUE...

The next scenario builds on the previous one we just looked at. Your interviewer will keep adding more conditions to the initial question to make it more complicated. It's a test to see how you juggle more pieces of information and how adept you are at quickly identifying relevant information.

As we work through the scenarios together, you'll see how the structure stays relatively the same despite the changes.

So there's no need to worry at all. Take it one step at a time and don't feel like you have to rush.

If you think you're taking too much time, you can say, "Sorry, I need a minute to compose my thoughts." Although, as I mentioned before, tutors want to hear your complete thought process. So thinking out loud can be beneficial to your overall interview performance.

NEGLIGENT SECOND DOCTOR

C ategory: Doctors

Tutor: Alright, let's say this time it's slightly different. Derek is affected by Anna's prescription and subsequently hits a pedestrian. But the pedestrian doesn't die and is instead seriously injured. When he gets to the hospital, he dies at the hands of a different doctor who messes up during surgery. Is Anna responsible for the death?

doctor (Anna) wrong meds -> patient (Derek) drives -> hits pedestrian -> negligent surgery -> pedestrian dies

Now our chain is more complicated. There are additional elements. You could write this out under your previous chain, making it easy to see the differences.

Let's get started! We'll focus on the new information

provided. Also, take note that the question asks for responsibility for the **death**, not the injury.

1. Possible answers

This is a little different from the last question because it highlights Anna specifically. Either Anna is responsible or she is not.

2. Analyzing Anna

A) From our previous analysis, we know Anna breached her duty as a doctor.

B) To determine whether Anna is responsible for the death, we need to ask whether Anna's actions contributed to the pedestrian's death.

- If not, then the pedestrian's death is on the second doctor. He wouldn't have died if the doctor didn't mess up. Anna would be liable for the serious injury only.
- If Anna's actions contributed to the death in any way, she would also be partially responsible for the death. Typically, she would be liable for less than the second doctor because that doctor is a more direct cause. A breakdown that could work is 33% to 67% for Anna and the second doctor, respectively.

When there's a chain of three or more elements, oftentimes the tutors want you to identify which parts of the chain are relevant. So being able to highlight the two hypotheticals is important.

EMPLOYEES, STRANGERS

INTRODUCING DUTIES AT WORK

E mployer-employee relationships are commonly discussed in law. There are only a few things you need to remember for your interview. More scenarios tend to centre around the employer's responsibilities.

Employers must:

- Provide a safe work environment (ex. protect against foreseeable risks) as established by the industry's standards
- Take responsibility for negligent acts of workers that occur during their course of employment

Employees must:

- Perform their duties to the established industry standards

1

WORKER FALLS ASLEEP

C ategory: Employer-Employee

Tutor: Carrie, a glassmaker, heats the furnace before leaving to attend a meeting across town. Before she left, she told her worker Fred to keep an eye on it. However, Fred ends up falling asleep, and the fire escapes the furnace and burns down the neighbour's wooden shed next door. Who should be blamed for the incident?

employer (Carrie) leaves fire -> worker (Fred) asleep -> neighbour's shed burns down

1. Possible answers

The two options for blame are Carrie and Fred, the employer and employee. Let's look at each of them in turn.

· · ·

2. Analyzing Fred, Carrie

One of the relevant breaches for Carrie relates to the negligent acts of workers. So let's start with Fred.

A) FRED: It's safe to say that sleeping on the job goes against most job descriptions. There's no exception for someone working at a glassmaking facility.

B) Again, it's pretty clear that Fred falling asleep is a negligent act. So there's not too much to analyze here.

- One way to perhaps defend Fred's behaviour is if he has a recognized medical condition such as chronic insomnia.

Alright, done with Fred. Let's jump back to Carrie.

A) CARRIE: As the employer, Carrie has to provide a safe work environment. The fire escaping the furnace can be construed as a foreseeable risk she failed to adequately contain (your tutor may counter this with new facts).

To summarize our analysis, Fred acted negligently while doing his assigned tasks during work hours. This means that Carrie, as his employer, must take responsibility for the damages.

B) Given that Fred is also significantly negligent, Carrie doesn't bear the full responsibility. The percentage breakdown depends on how badly Fred messed up by sleeping on the job.

Since his job relates to fire, a substance that could lead to disastrous consequences, you could reason that it's a fairly big mistake. You could argue that Fred should be responsible for something like 20% to 30% of the damages. It all depends on how you support the number you decide on.

INTRODUCING DUTIES OF STRANGERS

People often talk about the bystander effect and how strangers often will not help you. But the relevant question is whether strangers are legally obligated to help you.

Strangers must:

- Well, there's nothing they *must* do, generally speaking

Unless:

- There is a professional relationship where it is reasonably expected that they will help you (ex. your lawyer)
- The stranger has assumed responsibility for you (ex. an assigned caretaker)
- The stranger created the risk that harms you (ex. a trespasser started a fire in your house)

THE BLIND WOMAN

C ategory: Strangers

Tutor: Max is walking along the river and spots a blind woman walking towards him without a cane. As the two approach each other, Max notices a large hole directly in her path. It's clear that she will fall into it if he doesn't warn her. Is he obligated to warn her? If she falls in and hurts herself, is he responsible?

man (Max) doesn't warn stranger of danger -> she falls in hole + injury

The key aspect that differentiates this scenario from the previous one is the relationship between the two people involved.

1. Possible answers

There are two options here for each question. Either Max is obligated to warn her or he's not. Either Max is responsible for her injury or he's not.

2. Analyzing Max

For a question like this, rather than looking at hypotheticals like we've done so far, we're going to use perspectives.

A strong answer should be more substantial than just, "There is no obligation and responsibility because Max and the woman are mere strangers."

So you can split your explanation into two views to support your thinking, and we'll do that in (B).

A) Max has no duty to the blind woman, who is a mere stranger to him. It would be different if they were an employer-employee relationship, like the glassmaker scenario. So he has no obligation to warn her and wouldn't be responsible if she gets injured.

Also, Max didn't create the risk (the hole).

B) To complete our analysis, we must explain our previous answer using different perspectives. *Why should there be no obligation or responsibility?*

- Practical: In reality, rules (such as laws) must be carefully enforced, being mindful of the individual's freedom. Imposing the duty to rescue or protect others can be seen as an overreach, encroaching on one's right to choose what they are willing to do.
- Moral: What *should* be right can be subjective. But a general duty to prevent harm or help someone can apply to just about anyone, and

the limits are unclear and hard to determine. It would be unreasonable to apply such a duty.

The full explanation makes this a solid answer. Even if your opinion may be different, this is how your answer should be structured.

PART II

CAUSATION PART ONE

INTRODUCING CAUSATION

L et's talk about causation! It's a concept mentioned previously, and you've already started drawing those fancy chains to help illustrate scenarios. So this isn't an unfamiliar idea. If you venture beyond this book, you'll mostly see chains drawn for if-then and causation statements in logical reasoning textbooks.

Causation is a fascinating concept, with many exceptions. But for your interview, you only need to know several key ideas.

1. Hypotheticals don't matter: Only actions that occur matter.
2. Only foreseeable causes matter: If it's unforeseeable like a natural disaster, it makes little sense to blame anyone.
3. Eggshell: This idea is a bit complex. But basically, the law protects vulnerable victims even if it's unfair to the perpetrator. We'll expand more on the eggshell rule when we get to that scenario.

Right now, these bullet points may seem abstract. But the following scenarios will clear up your confusion. It's not complicated at all.

WATER FLASK

Category: Hypotheticals

Tutor: Ryan is walking through the desert with a water flask. Unbeknownst to him, his flask was tampered with twice when he wasn't paying attention. First, one vengeful enemy poisoned his water. Afterwards, another enemy poked a hole in the flask, emptying all the contents. Ryan ends up dying of dehydration. Who is to blame for his death?

enemy 1 poisons water -> enemy 2 pokes hole -> man (Ryan) dies of dehydration

Since this is a sequential relationship where one event happens after the other, make sure you have the correct order. The poisoning happens *before* the hole is created.

.   .   .

1. Possible answers

At first glance, we can see that our potential answers for blame are the first enemy, the second enemy, or both.

2. Analyzing both enemies

Since we have two enemies, let's analyze each separately.

A) ENEMY 1: The question is… how did Ryan die? Dehydration. Enemy 1's situation is a classic example of a hypothetical that didn't cause the eventual effect (death). The poisoning was not an active factor when Ryan died.

B) Enemy 1 poisoned the water, which is bad, but Ryan didn't die from being poisoned. He died from the lack of water.

- So Enemy 1 cannot be blamed.

A) ENEMY 2: From our analysis of Enemy 1, it's clear that dehydration is the key to finding the one to blame. Enemy 2's actions were not hypothetical and directly led to the effect.

B) Enemy 2 is the one who emptied the flask, effectively killing Ryan by depriving him of water.

- So Enemy 2 is the one to blame for Ryan's unfortunate ending.

––––––

Hypotheticals are quite intuitive. After all, it doesn't make sense for someone to take responsibility for something that didn't harm anyone.

UNFORTUNATE LIGHTNING

C ategory: Unforeseeable Events

Tutor: Sara drank a bottle of tequila before getting into her car to drive home. On the way home, she crashes into a parked truck on the curb. The driver of the truck, Lia, is non-fatally injured. While on the way to the hospital, Lia's ambulance is struck by lightning and she dies immediately. Should Sara be blamed for Lia's death?

inebriated (Sarah) car accident -> non-fatal injury (Lia) -> lightning strikes ambulance -> person dies

A chain of four looks more complicated, but the general ideas are the same.

In this scenario, we can safely presume that every event led to the next. Without the car accident, Lia wouldn't have gotten injured. Without the injury, she wouldn't have ended up in the ambulance.

Similar to one of the previous scenarios, notice that the scenario asks for blame concerning the **death**, not the injury.

1. Possible answers

Either Sarah is to be blamed or not to be blamed.

2. Analyzing the lightning

A) Whenever your scenario contains a natural event such as lightning, an earthquake, flooding, or fire, you should immediately ask yourself, "Is this a foreseeable event?"

- For instance, there are situations where a fire is unforeseeable, like when a random fireball falls from the sky. However, there are also situations where a fire is foreseeable, like our previous glassmaking scenario.

B) The lightning that hit the ambulance is not foreseeable. Without the lightning striking the ambulance, Lia would not have died since she was suffering from non-fatal injuries.

- Sarah should not be blamed for Lia's death.

———

Also pretty intuitive, right? Now let's look at a more complex situation…

INTRODUCING EXCEPTIONS

T he law is not exactly fair.
When faced with the victim and the perpetrator, the law prioritizes the victim. The law ensures
vulnerable or frail individuals are not disadvantaged when
seeking remedies for wrongdoing. The perpetrator may be
disproportionately on the hook due to this general rule.

Now what does the rule entail?

Particular characteristics that make the victim more
susceptible to injury cannot be used as a defence against
them.

- Say, for example, you have a weak heart. If
  you're assaulted and have a heart attack, the
  defendant cannot use the fact that you have a
  pre-existing heart condition to lessen their
  liability.

There are two key characteristics you should know.

1. Health Issues: The legal doctrine is called the
   "eggshell skull rule". Imagine a thin skull that's

like an eggshell. Because it's so thin, it's especially vulnerable to injury. If someone injured that skull, even without knowing about the vulnerability, they would still be liable for the entire injury.

2. Certain Religious Beliefs: Religious beliefs may prevent the victim from getting a blood transfusion that could've saved their life. If they end up dying, the defendant still cannot use the victim's religious beliefs as a defence.

TRANSFUSION

Category: Vulnerable Victims

Tutor: John pushes Carol out into oncoming traffic and she ends up seriously injured in the hospital. The doctor informs her that she'll need a blood transfusion for an urgent surgery to save her life. However, because of her religious beliefs, Carol refuses the blood transfusion. She subsequently dies. Is John responsible for her death?

man (John) injures victim (Carol) -> victim rejects transfusion b/c beliefs -> victim dies

You already know the answer because this scenario appears in our list of concepts to remember. But let's work through it using our typical structure.

1. Possible answers

Either John is responsible, or he's not.

2. *Analysis*

A) This is a classic case. When health issues or religious beliefs are brought up, you should instantly think back to this section.

B) When answering this type of question, support your answer with reasonable points. Let's look at two different perspectives.

- In a situation where John is not held responsible because of Carol's religious beliefs, that would mean religious people could be compensated unfairly less due to their beliefs.
- Now the opposite. If John is held responsible, the burden would be on the person who was in the wrong in the first place. Remember, Carol is the victim here. She shouldn't bear the burden, since she was the innocent party.

From the above analysis, it makes sense that John is responsible for Carol's death.

PART III

CAUSATION PART TWO

INTRODUCING CONCURRENCY IN
CAUSATION

W hat are concurrent causes?

Concurrent is defined as "operating or occurring at the same time".

- Merriam-Webster

Our previous chapter introduced causation scenarios. In this chapter, we're delving into several more complex ones. You should know these concepts, but it's not imperative that you do.

These scenarios have a bit more nuance. But as long as you know the general rules, you'll be fine.

Instead of having one cause leading to another, there are several **at the same time**.

Here are the types of scenarios we'll be studying in the following pages.

1. <u>Sufficient</u>: All the causes are, on their own, enough to lead to the effect (ex. 5 people, each applying lethal force to murder someone).

$$\begin{array}{c} \text{cause A} \searrow \\ \text{cause B} \rightarrow \text{effect} \\ \text{cause C} \nearrow \end{array}$$

2. <u>Cumulative:</u> Each cause alone is not enough to cause the effect, the effect is cumulative (ex. 100 people throwing small stones to knock down a wall).

$$\text{cause A} + \text{cause B} + \text{cause C} \rightarrow \text{effect}$$

Kind of abstract, right? Let's go through one scenario for each bullet point. Illustrating the concepts is the best way to study, after all.

HUNTERS IN THE WOODS

When you encounter scenarios with multiple concurrent causes, you may be presented with limited information. That way, your tutors can test whether you know when to ask the right questions.

C ategory: Sufficient Concurrent Causes

Tutor: There are two hunters in the woods with hunting rifles. Both of them spot rustling amongst the trees in the distance. Believing they've encountered a deer, both of them shoot a total of four bullets, two each. It turns out the movement in the trees came from another hunter. That hunter ends up dying from being shot. Who is to be blamed?

Here's the chain.

H1 ↘
injured

H2 ↗

This scenario is quite a popular one. You may have heard of it before.

The first step is to recognize that this scenario has multiple potential causes. Through asking additional questions and further analysis, we can figure out who to hold responsible.

1. Possible answers

There are three options. Either one of the hunters is liable and the other isn't, both are liable, or neither is liable.

2. Supporting our stance

A) Good questions to ask your interviewer include, "Is each bullet enough to kill the hunter?" and "Could they identify which bullet killed him?"

Now let's say your tutor tells you there is no way to identify who shot the fatal bullet.

That puts us firmly in the first point, the sufficient category, as listed in the introduction.

B) With one fatal bullet, a shot by either hunter is enough to kill. In this situation, both hunters should be liable. Why is that? Here's how to support this stance.

Let's go through the three possible answers and analyze the implications.

- If just one of the shooting hunters is liable, how would the liable one be chosen? Based on the current facts, there is no way to do that.
- If neither is liable, then the victim would get no

recuperation for being wronged. The victim is much worse off.
- The least unfair option for the deceased hunter would be for both of the remaining hunters to be jointly liable.

———

Remember, the law, if put to the test (as in, the ruling is unclear), tends to favour the plaintiff over the defendant. Those who are treated unfairly or wronged are prioritized.

LAKE POLLUTANTS

C ategory: Cumulative Concurrent Causes

Tutor: Four friends are hanging out by the lake with an assortment of paints. For fun, they decide to pour out the jars of paint into the lake. Friend A pours in two units, B pours in three units, C pours in three units, and D pours in four units. To be toxic, the lake would need eight units of pollutants. Who is responsible for polluting the lake?

A + B + C + D -> polluted lake

1. Possible answers

The options for responsibility are all the friends together, a subset of the friends, or none of them.

. . .

2. *Supporting our stance*

For many of our scenarios, we can assume the only relevant factors are the specific ones mentioned. For example, in this scenario, **it's likely built into the scenario that the lake was not previously polluted.** That's because the interviewer is trying to test this specific situation, so all else is assumed to be constant (if you've studied economics before, it's a similar idea to *ceteris paribus*).

A) You can acknowledge this idea by saying, "I'm going to assume that before the friends poured the paint into the water, the lake was not already polluted."

- It's fine to ask a question rather than leaping to the assumption.

It's clear that this scenario is cumulative, number two in our introduction.

B) We can approach this question similarly to the hunters one. Let's go over the implications of each of the three possible answers.

- If no one is responsible, then that comes across as super unfair. Malicious actors can take advantage of this loophole to get away with wrongdoings.
- Notice that certain subsets of the four friends exceed the minimum of eight units. For instance, friends B, C, and D add up to ten units. Friends A, C, and D add up to nine units. How would you determine which group is responsible? There's no way to do it.
- That leaves the last option, where everyone is equally responsible. The pollution of the lake will not go unpunished.

————

The analysis of the hunters and this lake pollutants scenario are both rather similar.

EVIDENCE

INTRODUCING THE POWER OF EVIDENCE

I n this section, scientific evidence reigns supreme.
We're going to quickly go over two evidence-based causation scenarios. These examples contain unknown causes. However, you may argue that the two previous scenarios in this section also contain unknown causes.

In a way, you are correct.

Which hunter shot the fatal bullet is unknown. Which combination of friends polluted the lake is also unknown. Our eventual conclusion to make everyone responsible is merely to ensure that misconducts are not left unpunished.

However, in this section, there is a key difference. **These scenarios are typically medical or scientific in nature.**

1. Indeterminate Cause: Given the facts of the scenario, there is not enough evidence to establish a cause. This can be due to other potential causes, etc.

2. Incapable of Finding a Cause: Based on modern scientific and medical knowledge, there

is no way to figure out if there's a causal link (ex. whether dust at a factory caused dermatitis can't be established based on medical knowledge).

The difference is subtle, but it's there. The first bullet point tackles medical/scientific cases with many potential causes thrown together, making it difficult to know which one affected the result. However, the other handles cases, often with diseases, where science is not advanced enough to pinpoint the answer.

The key to these types of scenarios is what the scientists and medical professionals are saying. So asking your interviewer about the evidence surrounding the cause is very important.

Also, both examples in this section stem from actual UK cases.

PREMATURE BABY

C ategory: Indeterminate Cause

Tutor: A baby is born prematurely and has to stay in the hospital for an extended period. In a breach of duty during that time, the hospital accidentally administered too much oxygen. The baby ends up with retrolental fibroplasia, a condition which leaves him with blindness in one eye and severe impairment in the other. Is the hospital responsible?

premature birth ↘
condition (blindness, etc)
hospital breach ↗

Remember that there are inherent risks relevant to a premature birth. Don't get distracted by the hospital's obvious breach.

. . .

1. Possible answers

Even if not explicitly stated, the facts of the scenario make it clear the hospital breached its duty towards its patient.

The possible answers are either the hospital is responsible for the baby's condition, or it's not.

2. Finding links

A) We need to see if we can establish links between the breach and the premature birth with retrolental fibroplasia (or RLF).

Here, you can turn to the interviewer.

After asking the tutor, he replies, "The baby's condition could be caused by either factors related to the premature birth or by the hospital's breach."

That tells us this is a scenario of indeterminate cause. There is no evidence that any of the potential causes are more likely than the others to lead to RLF.

B) What happens if we don't know the cause? There's no straightforward way to allocate blame in this situation. It could be from the lack of oxygen, but it could also be from complications because of premature birth.

Since pinning the responsibility on the hospital wouldn't make sense, the hospital is not responsible (despite the breach).

———

Remember that in this case, it's very possible nobody caused the baby's RLF. This is the major difference between these evidence scenarios and the ones we saw before. In both the hunters and the lake pollutants examples, it's abundantly clear someone did something wrong.

It's much more ambiguous here.

ASBESTOS

Category: Cannot Determine Causation

Tutor: Twenty-five years ago, John worked at a factory. His job responsibilities guaranteed asbestos exposure. Just recently, John was diagnosed with mesothelioma, an aggressive form of cancer. In the twenty years since he left his factory job, he'd worked at other places without asbestos, yet those environments may have also contributed to his eventual diagnosis. Is his factory employer responsible for his disease?

factory asbestos ↘
cancer (mesothelioma)
environ factors ↗

The name of the disease is not important.

. . .

1. Possible answers

The question specifically asks about the factory employer. Either the employer is responsible or they're not.

2. Finding links

A) First, we need to know about the link between asbestos and mesothelioma. This is a good time to ask a question, and you could word it like this, "Is there a causal link between the factory's asbestos exposure and that type of cancer?"

Now let's say your interviewer tells you it's not possible to determine whether the asbestos fibre from the employer's factory caused John's cancer.

- However, she also tells you the experts confirmed that the work asbestos exposure increased the risk of the disease by 5%.

So we know that we're looking at the second bullet point from the introduction, incapable of finding a cause.

B) We've gained quite a lot of information in (A). Now we have to put it all together.

- Let's say the employer is responsible. That would make sense if we **didn't** know about the 5% increased risk since it would be unfair to deny John a remedy. But the 5% is too small to be significant.
- That leaves us with the employer not being responsible.

———

To repeat the above, if the tutor didn't further inform you about the 5% increased risk, the employer would be on the hook. Unlike the previous scenario where we couldn't pinpoint the cause due to other possible causes, in this case, **it's impossible to find the cause**. The interviewer also clarified that working at the factory did increase the risk of disease. These two facts would make the employer responsible.

However, knowing the risk increased by only 5% makes the employer not liable. And why is the 5% not enough to demonstrate causation? Our next section will go into further detail on that.

PART IV

LOST OPPORTUNITIES

INTRODUCING LOST OPPORTUNITIES

L et's talk about percentages and chances!
Don't worry, no maths yet! That's in the section where we talk about remedies. Right now, let's focus on concepts related to lost opportunities.

For your interview, there are two scenarios to keep in mind. Both relate to the medical profession yet again. Since you're not expected to know any legal concepts in your interview, tutors bring up everyday events such as drivers and doctors because you know those topics well.

1. <u>Doctor:</u> A doctor fails to warn their patient about a risk related to an operation or a side effect.

2. <u>Hospital:</u> Due to a breach of duty, a patient is treated later than they could have been. This may have been a doctor's breach as well. But for the sake of comparison, we'll call it a hospital's breach.

- With these scenarios, ask for information

regarding the percentage chance of the injury happening **without negligence**.

Alright, let's hop right into illustrating these two points! There are several additional concepts that you'll learn by reading through the examples.

PARALYSIS RISK

C ategory: Doctors

Tutor: Anna, a doctor, is prescribing medicine to treat Max. She didn't warn Max about the risk of paralysis, which is a side effect of the medicine. After proper, regular use of the medicine, Max ends up with nerve damage and partial paralysis. Is Anna to blame?

doctor fails to warn of risk -> risk happens

This chain may seem too abstract. Chains and notes are to remind you of the question details as you answer questions from your interviewer. So write whatever makes sense to you.

Alright, this scenario is rather short.

1. Possible answers

Either Anna is responsible, or she's not responsible. Partial responsibility appears unlikely since Max used the medicine properly.

2. Percentage analysis

A) You could be tempted to ask about the likelihood of paralysis as a side effect. That's fine.

- Your tutor tells you there is a 1% chance of paralysis from using the medicine.

From what we learned in the "Breach of Duty" chapter, you know that failing to warn of a risk that impacts medical decision-making is a breach of duty.

B) Another aspect your tutor could point out is the 1% risk appears quite low. While that may be true, that's not relevant in this scenario.

- What's important here is that Max's injury is a product of the very risk Anna failed to warn. While Max's reaction to hearing about the risk cannot be predicted, Anna should've done her job correctly.

Therefore, yes, Anna is responsible.

2

DELAYED TREATMENT

C ategory: Percentage Chance Pre-Incident

Tutor: Finn fell from a ladder while he was trying to put ornaments on the top of the giant Christmas tree in his front yard. He goes to the hospital where the doctor fails to treat his injured hip on time. Finn ends up with necrosis and a long-term disability. Is the hospital responsible for the development of his injuries?

delayed treatment -> patient disabled

Since the tutor didn't specify between the doctor and hospital, you can assume they're the same.

1. Possible answers
Either the hospital is responsible or they aren't.

· · ·

2. Percentage analysis

A) As we mentioned in the introduction, we must ask about the percentage chance of the injury happening if Finn was treated within the proper timeframe.

- Your interviewer says, "If Finn was diagnosed and treated correctly, he would have a 75% chance of developing a disability."

That's enough information for us to form our final answer.

B) The 75% makes a very big difference here. Let's look at two hypotheticals with different percentages.

- If the percentage was less than 50%, Finn would've been more likely to **not** end up with his disability.
- If the percentage is higher than 50%, which it is, the 75% risk was already there at the time he fell. The jump from 75% to 100% (which represents what happened) is not significant enough to warrant responsibility.

After our analysis, it is established that the hospital is not responsible for Finn's injuries.

———

You can see that the percentage matters less in the paralysis scenario compared to this hospital breach one. The percentage determines the right answer here.

THE REST OF THE BOOK

The rest of the book will target questions that have less structured answers. Instead, there's more subjectivity with no exact answer. You'll need to form a well-structured argument that your interviewer may counter.

So we won't be using the answer structure we've been using before. Instead, each chapter will outline its structure in the introduction. You'll also notice that we're moving away from the categories highlighted in the reference table at the start of the book.

For the scenarios, if applicable, I'll continue to provide examples of questions you could ask your interviewer.

PART V

MURDER

INTRODUCING MURDER

W hat is murder? How are murder and morality interconnected?

When interviewers ask you about these scenarios, they want to see you think more analytically. The balance between the "right" thing to do and what happens in the real world can feel perplexing.

But before we jump into the scenarios, here is the definition of murder.

Murder is intentionally causing the death of another person.

Again, you're not expected to know the official legal definition. So just this is enough. But let's break down the other more complicated terms in that sentence.

If someone has intent, it means they desire the consequence that follows their action.

Causation refers to a situation where an action leads to a consequence.

Knowing these definitions will help you decipher whether a given scenario depicts murder. But whether a perpetrator *should* be guilty of murder asks for your opinion. With subjective questions, don't stick to any definitions and showcase your independent thinking.

For each scenario in this section, the answers will be structured as follows:

1. Given the facts of the case, is the action necessary?
2. Based on the definition, is this murder?
3. *Should* the defendant be guilty of murder?

Necessity, like murder, has a complicated legal definition you're not expected to know. For the purposes of your interview, whether an action is necessary can be assessed by the criteria below.

1. Is there a real, urgent need?
2. Was there another, less extreme option that could lead to a better result?

These two points are taken out of the defence of necessity, which we'll use to structure an answer in one of the following scenarios. Our analysis for each scenario is slightly different, demonstrating several ways to structure your answer to these subjective questions.

The examples we'll go through are fairly well-known and occasionally show up in lists containing thought experiments.

CONJOINED TWINS

This scenario will serve as an example of the structure of the answers for all the others in this chapter.

Tutor: Sam and Sally are conjoined twin toddlers with a medical condition. If the doctor doesn't separate them, both twins will die. However, if he separates them, one will live and the other will die. If the doctor separates the twins, are his actions considered murder?

separate twins -> one dies
~~**separate twins**~~ **-> both die**

A question that you may ask is, "Did the parents agree to the operation?"

Your interview replies, "No."

- Is this answer relevant to our following analysis? You can argue that it doesn't because it's not uncommon for the government to step in to protect the well-being of children.

1. Is the action necessary?

If the doctor didn't separate them, both Sam and Sally would die. If the doctor separated them, he would save one of them.

Choosing to separate is the necessary action here. The alternative leads to a much worse outcome.

2. Is this murder?

This scenario fits the definition of murder completely. If the surgery happens, the doctor would be intentionally committing an act that would certainly lead to a person's death.

3. Should the doctor be guilty of murder?

Now here's when your opinion comes in. As long as you can strengthen your answer with sound evidence, you can hold any opinion. However, I advise you to choose an idea that is easier to support. No matter what you say, be prepared for the tutor to push back on your thinking.

Let's argue that the doctor should **not** be guilty of murder. We'll structure our answer based on the legal defence of necessity.

- Could be worse: The surgery is done to avoid a worse situation, which is both twins dying.
- No alternative: The only way to separate the

twins is through surgery. It's impossible to find a less extreme method to solve the issue.

- Intentions: The benefits of acting outweigh not acting. In a way, you can see the surgery as "saving someone" versus "killing someone".

For similar types of scenarios, you can use the underlined parts of the bullet points above to frame your answer.

PRISONER'S ORGANS

Tutor: Liam is a very sickly prisoner in a coma, and doctors are certain that he will not live past the next two months. Six people are currently in the hospital, urgently waiting for organs. If Liam is killed, his organs could be used to save all of these people. Is this murder? And should it be allowed?

kill one dying prisoner -> saves seven people

This question has moral elements because of the "should". So the fact that Liam is a prisoner is relevant.

1. Is the action necessary?

Killing someone is an extreme option. Looking at our criteria, let's ask some questions. You ask your interviewer, "Is it likely that those waiting for organs will get organs through proper channels soon?"

The tutor replies, "They all need organ transplants within the next two weeks or they will die."

While this may pass as "urgent", is there a real medical need to murder one to save six?

- It can be argued that there will never be an absolute, enforceable medical need to kill someone, even a sickly individual. We'll delve into more of the details in the last part of our answer.

2. Is this murder?

Well, yes. It's murder because it's the intentional killing of a person.

3. Should this situation be allowed?

Now here's the loaded question where the bulk of the answer should focus on. We can split our analysis into three issues by picking apart every aspect of the scenario. The points below support the idea that this type of killing should **not** be allowed.

- Prisoner: Does being a prisoner mean you don't have bodily autonomy? Does it mean a prisoner's life is less valuable? Absolutely not, to both questions. Liam is in a coma and has no way of voicing his opinions on being killed to save others.
- Dying: Morally speaking, perhaps there should be a duty to preserve life. Murdering Liam when he still has life to live is not the right thing to do.

- <u>Killing for organs:</u> Liam may not have decided on whether he wants to donate his organs at all. And murdering someone for their organs could lead to undesirable consequences. How would doctors decide who should be sacrificed? Creating a hierarchy feels distasteful in a society which strives for equality and the preservation of life.

During your interview, it's fine to have only two points. After all, your nerves might kick in and you could find it tough to organize your thinking into a coherent answer.

LADDER ON A SINKING SHIP

Tutor: Jared is trying to escape a sinking ship. The water is rapidly rising and the escape route can only be accessed by climbing a ladder to the next floor. Unfortunately, there is a woman in the way, unwilling to move from her spot. Behind you, there are ten more people on the ladder, waiting to evacuate. If Jared pushes that woman off the ladder, would his actions be murder?

push woman -> saves ten
push~~ woman~~ -> all die

This is essentially what's being suggested in the scenario. But if you're unsure, you can ask more questions.

You might ask, "Were there any other options to remove the woman from the ladder? For instance, did Jared warn the woman repeatedly?"

Your interviewer replies, "Jared did ask her to move, but she refused."

1. Is the action necessary?

Based on the interview's answer above, it seems like Jared's actions would be necessary to save the group of people's lives. And there were no alternatives.

2. Is this murder?

To determine whether it is murder, let's figure out the intent.

You could ask your interviewer, "Did Jared know that if he pushed the woman, she would likely die?"

He says, "Given the speed of the rising water in the level everyone was stuck on, Jared knew that anyone who fell into the water would die."

Okay. So Jared committed murder.

3. Should Jared be guilty of murder?

This is where it gets tricky. Let's analyze this scenario closely. There are quite a few points you can bring up to argue that Jared should **not** be guilty of murder.

- No selection problem: Jared did not specifically pick out the woman to push. She was there already, by chance.
- Attempts to find an alternative: Jared didn't push her off without trying to ask her to move first. Since climbing the ladder was the only way out, there wouldn't be any other alternatives other than having her move.
- Urgency: Water was swiftly rising and soon everyone would be submerged if Jared didn't make the decision quickly. This was a do-or-die situation.

- <u>High numbers:</u> Jared would save ten people, which is not an insignificant number of people.

There are similarities to the previous murder-for-organs scenario. One imperative difference is timing. The patients in the organs scenario have weeks left. With Jared, he has seconds, maybe minutes.

———

One more thing to point out here. Let's say the interviewer replied differently in (2). The conversation went like this instead:

You ask, "Did Jared know that if he pushed the woman, she would likely die?"

He replies, "All Jared was thinking about was getting her out of the way so they could escape. He didn't think that far."

With this exchange, you can point out one more thing.

- Jared's intent was not to murder, but to remove her from the ladder and prevent ten deaths. It's possible that, even if he took the time to think about it, he'd assume she could swim and climb the ladder herself after falling into the water.

4

CANNIBALISM

Tutor: A captain, sailor, and cabin boy are in a lifeboat, floating on the open sea after their boat capsized. They desperately need help, but as time passes, they get more and more hopeless. When facing starvation, the captain and sailor kill the cabin boy and eat him. Is this murder? If not, should the captain and sailor be guilty of murder?

three face starvation -> two kill the cabin boy + eat him

You could think to ask, "How did they pick to eat the cabin boy? Was it random?"

Your interviewer says, "He was the sickest one out of all three. The other two decided without informing him."

Oof. The cabin boy didn't stand a chance.

Alright, let's jump in.

1. Are the actions necessary?

Is it necessary for the other two to murder and eat the

cabin boy? A better question would be, is it necessary to kill someone when you're starving?

This is a subjective question, and we're going to say no. Starvation is not an excuse for murder. That's a pretty reasonable stance, don't you agree?

If you don't agree, imagine thirty minutes after they killed the cabin boy, a commercial vessel happens to come by and save them.

- The cabin boy would very likely still be alive if he wasn't eaten.
- Even if the other two reasonably believed that they weren't getting saved anytime soon, they had no right to deny the cabin boy the slight possibility of staying alive.

2. Is this murder?

The captain and sailor conspired to kill the cabin boy, so they could have something to eat. It is clearly murder.

3. Should the two men be guilty of murder?

Similar to the previous scenario, there are many points you can make. We'll argue that they **should** be guilty of murder.

- Selection problem: The captain and sailor decided to end the cabin boy's life. It appears he was picked specifically, which is unfair.
- No consent: There was no conversation or agreement from the victim.
- Unreasonable grounds: As we said in (1), they

could be rescued right after. There are no reasonable grounds to believe that murdering one would save the other two. They could also never be saved.

- <u>Bad societal message:</u> If the captain and sailor are ruled not guilty, the judicial system would be sending problematic messages. They would be encouraging killing too soon, which effectively lowers the value of human life.

———

It probably seems tough to come up with these bullet points on the spot during your interview.

Here's a tactic. You can try to brainstorm points by thinking of three types of answers.

1. Targeting the concept of the scenario ("killing someone because you are starving is wrong").
2. Targeting the process of the scenario ("specifically choosing the youngest, sickest person to kill is not fair and shows malicious intent").
3. Targeting the implications of the answer you're arguing against (what we did in the last point above).

PART VI

CONTRACT VALIDITY

INTRODUCING CONTRACTS

O ther than doctors, drivers, and murder, what concepts are you exposed to during daily life?

This chapter focuses on contracts. Although you won't necessarily need the below explainer for the following scenarios, it can help you if the tutor gives you a more complex contractual case.

Now what exactly is a contract? We want to define it in layman's terms.

A contract is an agreement comprising an offer, consideration, and acceptance between parties.

The one word that looks confusing is "consideration", which is a legal term. What is that?

Consideration is what's given by a party in exchange for a promise (contract).

For example, Quinn's sister will give him candy if he helps her study for her test. The candy is the consideration.

The promise (or the contract) is the agreement between Quinn and his sister to help her study.

There isn't much of a structure for these scenarios. Instead, keep an eye on the underlined words in the explanations. Those are important points for you to remember.

In the first scenario, we'll cover concepts related to misrepresentation. But you won't need to use that term in your interview because you're not expected to know it. The specifics of what you should learn will be covered as we go through the examples.

This is a rather short chapter.

BUYING A VAN

T utor: Liam buys a van from Peter after hearing about its descriptions. Liam expected the car to be five years old. Peter told him the parts were easy to source from large chain stores. After buying it, Liam discovers the van is actually much older. An expert values the car at £28,000. He bought it for £40,000 and expected it to have been worth £53,000. After researching further, Liam learned that the sole company that sold parts had gone bankrupt. Is Peter liable for misleading Liam on the sale?

£28,000 car, purchased £40,000, expected £53,000

Calculations are not expected in this question. If you're ever expected to do calculations, the numbers would be round. It's a law interview after all, not a maths one.

From the first sentence, we can safely assume that Liam depended on Peter's statements when deciding whether to purchase the van. Another way to phrase this is that Liam wouldn't have purchased the car without Peter's descriptions.

1. Did Peter make false statements?
  First, let's highlight what Peter said about the van.

- The parts are easy to source.
- Specifically, easy to source from large chain stores.

Please note that Liam **expected** the car to be five years old. We're going to assume that Peter didn't explicitly say the car's age.

We'll look at two aspects when determining whether Peter made false statements (i.e. committed misrepresentation).

- <u>Timing:</u> There was a gap between the time of the sale and when Liam did further research. Perhaps Peter was telling the truth at the time, and large chain stores stopped selling those parts sometime after the car was sold, but before Liam found out.
- If, prior to the sale's completion, Peter found out about the lack of supply, he *is* liable for misleading Liam. The responsibility still existed up until the van exchanged hands.
- <u>Opinion:</u> If Peter was just giving his opinion, and he was not expected to know anything about sourcing parts for the van, he was not making a false statement.

- This one is a bit iffy. As a seller of the van, it can easily be argued that Peter should have information about purchasing parts.

During the interview, you can ask questions concerning these two ideas to see where the interviewer is trying to lead you.

Example question: "Did the large chain stores previously supply parts?"

2. The age

Obviously, the age of a car sold is very relevant to the sale. But in this case, Liam believed the car was five years old without Peter's input.

Let's look at two scenarios here.

- Liam brought up the age during negotiations, and Peter didn't correct him.
- Liam didn't mention the age at all, and Peter didn't bring it up either.

In either case, Peter is not in the wrong. As long as Peter didn't actively try to make Liam believe the car was younger than it was, he would not be liable for Liam's incorrect belief.

Silence is not a statement. If silence is considered a statement and Peter is therefore held liable, then that leaves the door open for more disputes and potential litigation in other cases. These consequences are undesirable because they waste resources.

. . .

3. Conclusion

There are many moving parts in this scenario which require questions and answers between you and your interviewer. Follow their lead as you work through the scenario, speak out loud, and you'll be just fine.

WE'RE FAMILY

Tutor: A mother promises her daughter to support her financially if she studies law in the UK. Her daughter was previously living abroad elsewhere. When her daughter agreed, the mother bought her a house in London. After an argument, the mother withdrew her support. Is her daughter entitled to stay in the house?

withdraw family promise -> remedy?

This is a pretty well-known case taught during the first year of a law degree. Whether the initial promise and acceptance are collectively a contract is not relevant. What this question is asking is whether family promises should be legally binding.

As for most "should" questions, there are quite a few ways you can support your argument. The below break-down brings up several points you could consider bringing up when structuring your answer.

. . .

1. Introduction

You can start by mentioning that the daughter uprooted her life because of the mother's promise. She depended on this agreement to make major life changes.

2. Family Contracts or Agreements

Some people may find it hard to find a stance on whether family promises should be legally enforceable. There are several ways to structure your answer, and you can start by touching on several of the points below.

- Reality: If you think about your daily interactions with your own family, you'll see there is rarely actual intention to make a legal agreement. Familial promises are built on a foundation of trust, and the law should not interfere.
- Increased litigation: There would be increased litigation which would redirect resources from more serious and important cases in the legal system. The social repercussions could potentially be very significant. If family promises are subject to litigation, then in theory, pretty much anything can be held liable.
- Social purpose: The law and society want to promote good faith in relationships, not relationships with the threat of litigation constantly hanging over them.

3. Conclusion

Note that in the actual law, family promises are not

legally binding. I recommend you take the common stance in your arguments simply because it's easier to argue and your interviewer's mind is already primed to accept that answer.

However, the most important factor is that you need to feel confident about stating your points and can anticipate pushback from your interviewer.

PART VII

REMEDIES

INTRODUCING REMEDIES

W e mentioned back in the Breach of Duty chapter that monetary remedies could be a concern during your interview. It's prudent to look at how exactly those numbers are calculated.

Throughout the book, we've already got the percentages down, so now it's time to translate those percentages to actual monetary values. It's fine to just say something like "20% of £200,000", but where did that £200,000 come from? That's what we're going to focus on during this section.

There are two remedy scenarios we'll look at.

1. Death: Take, for example, our scenario mentioned in the Breach of Duty section concerning a doctor prescribing the wrong medicine leading to their patient driving irresponsibly and killing a pedestrian.

2. Serious Injury: We also previously talked about the difference between responsibility for death and serious injury. In other words, total loss of earnings versus earnings reduced due to injury,

respectively. The second situation is more complicated than the first one.

For either scenario, you have to remember the factors needed to calculate the monetary compensation number.

1. <u>Age at date of trial:</u> Calculations are not made based on the date of injury or death.

2. <u>Sex:</u> Women are expected to work less.

3. <u>Level of education attainment:</u> none, A-levels only, degree, etc.

4. Pre- and post-accident

- <u>Disabled status</u>
- <u>Earning capacity</u>
- <u>Expected retirement age</u>

If you're curious about how everything is actually calculated, look up Ogden Tables.

1

LIABLE FOR DEATH

Remedy questions tend to come up after you've already analyzed the scenario. It comes at the end before your interview moves to another scenario.

So here we go.

YOU: The doctor is 75% liable for Adam's death.

TUTOR: Okay. What information do you need to know to figure out how much money the doctor is liable for?

Below, you'll see an example of a back-and-forth with the interviewer.

1. Information to know
All the information needed is listed in the introduction.

Since this is a death scenario, you'll focus on the pre-accident factors only.

So the answer includes age, sex, education level, previous expected retirement age, previous earning capacity, and previous disabled status.

————

TUTOR: Good. Adam would be aged 40 at the age of trial. He wasn't disabled, had no education attainments and made £20,000 a year. He planned to retire when he was 60. How much should the doctor have to be liable for?

————

2. Calculations

You don't have to be a mathematician. And if you looked at the Ogden Tables, you'd notice that it's tough to mentally do calculations with those multipliers and adjustment factors.

Here are the things to bring up:

- The doctor is required to compensate for the £20,000 a year Adam would've earned during the span of his working years. This would be discounted to the present value, so the number here would be less than the value of £20,000 x 21.

- The value must be adjusted down further to take into account that Adam may not have spent all his working ages actually working. Since he had no education attainments, he would've worked slightly less than someone who had a degree, for example.

So you could take this into account by multiplying the discounted answer of (£20,000 x 21) by 0.80.

I did base the 0.80 from the relevant Ogden Tables used to calculate remedies for actual UK cases. That can be the baseline number you use and adjust upwards and downwards based on the facts of the scenario you get.

3. The percentage breakdown

The doctor is liable for 75%. Take that final number in the second step and multiply by 0.75.

4.. Last point

Your interviewer is not expecting you to know specific numbers. But whatever numbers you throw out there should be backed with a logical explanation.

LIABLE FOR SERIOUS INJURY

S CENARIO: Serious Injury

YOU: The doctor is completely liable for Carol's paralysis.

TUTOR: Alright, what do you need to know to calculate the doctor's monetary liability for the patient's injury?

Unlike the first scenario, we'll have pre- and post-numbers. It makes the calculation a tad bit more complicated because you have to do subtraction.

1. Information to know
    We'll need to know Carol's age, sex, education level, and pre- and post-accident expected retirement age, earning capacity, and disabled status.

———

TUTOR: Carol is now disabled but she can still work. However, her expected retirement age is now 63, before it was 65. She is 30 years old and has a bachelor's degree. Her earnings post-injury are £6,000 a year and her earnings pre-injury were £18,000 a year.

———

2. Calculations

When the amount of earnings decreases post-injury, remember to take what the victim would've earned and subtract the amount of new earnings. You want to only account for what the victim lost out on.

So we can separate Carol's calculations into three parts. Her pre-paralysis earnings, her post-paralysis earnings, and the subtraction.

1. Take the discounted value of £18,000 for 36 years. She wasn't disabled before and had a degree, so this number wouldn't be adjusted much. Maybe multiply by 0.85.
2. Then let's handle her earnings post-injury. Take the discounted value of £6,000 for 34 years. Carol is now disabled, so this value will be adjusted by a significant amount. Let's say multiply by 0.45.
3. Subtract the values from both sections to get the amount the doctor is liable for.

3. Last point

Don't worry about missing any aspects of the calculation step. If you get lost, your interviewer will help guide you there.

Remember, your interview is intended to be a mock tutorial. The tutor wants to see how you react to their guidance and adapt to changes. So stay calm. It's alright to stop and think through your answer before speaking.

AFTERWORD

Getting into Oxbridge may seem like a daunting task. There's no magical formula to succeeding in the interview, but the one thing you can do is prepare as much as you can.

Confidence is important, as is your quick thinking.

Hopefully, *The Oxbridge Law Interview Tiny Handbook* helped you gain clarity on your interview.

Good luck with your LNAT if you haven't already taken it! A high result on the LNAT secures your interview, even if you feel like the rest of your application is lacklustre. Don't stress on the essay. Read up on current events so you have some wide-ranging topics to support your arguments.

You're likely to be asked one or two questions about something on your personal statement, so know your story.

Thank you for reading the *Tiny Handbook*, and all the best to you!

ABOUT THE AUTHOR

When not thinking about the law, Leo Miles is a lover of philosophy, economics, and hot tea. Before law, he had experience in the banking sector. He enjoys quality time with his dog and reading widely.

The *Tiny Handbook* is Miles' first book.

Contact Miles through email: leomilesbooks@mail.com

Made in the USA
Middletown, DE
15 September 2024